LEGACY
The Story of Nikola Tesla

By

Norma Brody

BookSurge Publishing
North Charleston, South Carolina

BookSurge Publishing
North Charleston, South Carolina

Printed in the United States of America
First Printing April 2008

Library of Congress Cataloguing-in-Publication Data
Library of Congress Control Number: 2008901264

Brody, Norma
Legacy: The Story of Nikola Tesla/Norma Brody

ISBN: 1-4196-8725-5

EAN13: 978-1419687259

TABLE OF CONTENTS

Chapter		Page
1	The Early Years	1
2	Dane's Death	7
3	A Move to Gospic	11
4	Nikola Is Very Sick	17
5	Working	25
6	Tesla and Westinghouse	35
7	Disaster Strikes	45
8	Worldwide Recognition	51
9	The Johnsons' House Party	55
10	Wardenclyffe Broadcasting	61
11	Controversial Issues	65
12	Tesla's Financial Crisis	71
Suggested Reading		79

LIST OF ILLUSTRATIONS

One of the Original Tesla Electric Motors (1888)	24
Tesla with Wireless Light Bulb	44
Interior of Power House No. 1 of the Niagara Falls Power Company (1895 – 1899)	50
Experimental Station at Colorado Springs	50
Transmitting Tesla Tower and Laboratory (NY)	64
Tesla's Funeral on January 12, 1943	77
Tesla's Statue on Goat Island, Niagra Falls, NY	78
Tesla Commemorative Plaque located on the Hotel New Yorker	78

LEGACY

With Special Thanks to
Alan H. Brody for his collaboration
and production design.

Chapter 1

THE EARLY YEARS

Bolts of lightning are cracking across the sky and thunder is rolling. It's midnight on July 10, 1856. We are in Smiljan, Yugoslavia, and there is a cry from a newborn baby.

The cuckoo clock on the wall indicates twelve o'clock, and the bird is coming out to sound the final three cuckoos. A candle flickers in the downstairs rooms of the two-story house.

The plump, middle-aged, graying woman wearing a white cotton cap is the midwife. She is all smiles as she presents the baby to its mother. "Mrs. Tesla, you have a beautiful baby boy. I will go tell Reverend Tesla, and I want you to get some rest."

Djourka Tesla, exhausted, but so happy, says, "What a good sign, to be born on a night like this."

Reverend Milutin Tesla is carrying a Bible and praying. He is the reverend for a church close to his house and has a very devoted congregation. The midwife says, "Your wife and son are waiting for you." He breaks from his prayers, and a look of excitement brightens his face. He says to the midwife, "It's an old wives' tale that a baby born in a thunderstorm has special gifts."

He puts down his Bible and heads for the bedroom.
Excited, he says to his wife, "We have created another
miracle. How are you feeling?"

"I think we are both doing just fine." The newborn is
snuggled comfortably in her arms and is sleeping quietly.
The house is warm and well-furnished, with many books.
Reverend Tesla, in his robe and slippers, takes the baby.
He has a huge smile on his face as he tells it, "You will be
very happy in this family. We will name you Nikola."

And so, Nikola becomes the fifth child in a family already
consisting of Dane, an older brother, and three older sisters:
Angelina, Mikla, and Marica.

* * *

A loaf of freshly cut bread is on the table, and the plates in
front of the boys hold only small crumbs. Nikola is now
four years old and Dane is eleven. They are sitting with
two of their older sisters -- and there is a high chair against
the wall. indicating a younger child who is not present.

Djourka's fantastic needlework has been neatly placed on a
table near the comfortable chair where she works. A
spinning wheel is in a corner, with a basket of various
colors of dyed wool sheared from their sheep.

Nikola is watching his mother tinker, trying to fix a toy.
She is showing a creative solution to a problem he's had
with the toy, which has stopped working. He is getting
impatient. "But, Mama, I'm through with the toy. I can
play with something else."

"Nikola," says his mother, "we must look for ways of making this work better. It's a challenge and there's much enjoyment left in this."

Nikola looks at her with fascination while she tinkers, then she smiles and hands him the toy. His eyes light up as he jumps off his chair and kisses her.

Nikola turns to Dane and says, "Come on, let's go outside and play with this now." Dane follows Nikola out of the kitchen. Mrs. Tesla puts away the few tools, walks to the window, and watches the boys as they run outside and play with their newly-repaired toy.

Their farm has a horse, cows, and geese, as well as the family's cat, Macak. The farm is nestled near a wooded area that gives the children many opportunities to enjoy their surroundings. Nikola often tries to ride the cow. The geese love to chase the children. Of all the animals, Macak is Nikola's favorite.

Nearby there is a stream with a waterwheel. Nikola gets an idea. He catches some mosquitoes, puts a sticky substance on them, and pastes them to the waterwheel. As they flap their wings trying to escape, the force of their struggling causes the waterwheel to start to turn. It is a wonderful experiment and Nikola is very excited with his success.

A few days later, Niko (as the family calls him) and Dane are playfully swimming and attempting to catch frogs. They're enjoying the challenge the frogs offer as they dart just out of reach. "Come on, Dane. Let's go look at the waterwheel." Both boys are laughing as they wander downstream to the smooth waterwheel.

Dane turns to Nikola and tells him, "This is creating energy for the farm over there."

Nikola asks, "What happens when the creek freezes over?"

"Gee, I don't know, Niko. We'll have to find out."

Even though there is seven years difference in their ages, they love spending the days together and are always adventurous. The children are trusted to venture into the woods, and they know where there are ponds with frogs in them and old, abandoned farmhouses. They are familiar with the noises of the woods and have learned to detect animals if any are close by.

* * *

It is evening, and the children are sitting on the floor by a roaring fire in the fireplace. Reverend Tesla is reading passages from the Bible aloud. He reads the fourth verse of Psalm 47 to them.

> *His lightning enlightened the world,*
> *The earth saw and trembled.*
> *The hills melted like wax at the presence of the Lord,*
> *At the presence of the Lord of the World.*

Reverend Tesla has mastered English, French, German, and Italian, and encourages his children to learn other languages.

Djourka reads a poem titled "Who Has Seen the Wind?"

> *Who has seen the wind?*
> *Neither you nor I.*
> *But when the trees bow down their heads,*
> *The wind is passing by.*

Everyone is listening intently. Dane says, "We're learning literature in school."

Djourka responds, "It's important to read the words of others through different voices."

Nikola interjects, "I wonder if I could write something."

Djourka looks at him, smiling. "Of course you can. Write down your feelings and what you see and what you think about. It's very important. As you grow older, it's a good way to remember things of the past."

She closes her book. "And we will continue to learn other people's languages." She gives each of the children a hug. "Now, off to bed."

Often, after everyone has gone to bed, Nikola tiptoes downstairs to the library, puts a cloth next to the opening at the bottom of the door, and reads by candlelight. He has never been caught and he certainly gets a lot of reading done.

In his visionary ideas Tesla was so far ahead of his time. Somebody said that Tesla was working on "inventing the future". He was a pioneer in many fields, but commonly misunderstood. His work paved the way for widespread electrification and information technology, and forever changed our lives.

Chapter 2

DANE'S DEATH

Dane and Nikola are outside. Dane is now twelve and Nikola is five. Djourka is preparing a family meal, and today appears like any other day. But it isn't.

Nikola is watching Dane ride his horse. He is an excellent horseman. Suddenly, Dane's horse rears and he is thrown to the ground, hitting his head. Nikola comes running and yells, "Dane! Dane!" When he reaches him, Dane is not moving. Nikola quickly runs into the house. "Mama, something has happened to Dane!"

Djourka runs outside with her apron on and leaves everything as it is in the kitchen.

A few days later, the family is at the gravesite. Reverend Tesla speaks, and then they lower Dane into the ground. Everyone is crying and comforting each other. Nikola is trying to hold back his tears. No words are spoken as everyone returns to the house.

Dane's death leaves an indelible memory in Nikola, and for many years he sees it again in his nightmares.

* * *

A year later, when Nikola is six years old, he comes across a running stream. He puts his hand in the water and strokes it in a downward motion.

He searches for some wood and finds a rough-cut wooden disk left behind from a lumbering operation. He cuts a hole through its center and forces a somewhat straight branch through it, which he rests in two sticks after forcing the branch into two rocks on either side of the brook.

The lower part of the disk rests in the water and the currents forces it to turn. He finds endless pleasure in watching his crude device derive power from the brook.

His boundless curiosity becomes a very important part of his life.

Later that year, Nikola and his father hike into the forest. They are sitting on a log. His father is instructing Nikola on how to create and maintain clear, visual images in his mind.

Gesturing with his hand, he says to Nikola, "Think of a ball. Think of a globe, a ball, a large, colored ball. Close your eyes if you need to."

Nikola says, "I'm closing my eyes."

"That's fine," says Reverend Tesla, "There, can you picture it?"

"I see a big blue ball. It's slowly turning," says Nikola, excited. He wrinkles his brow in deep concentration.

"Now what do you see?" asks Reverend Tesla.

"I'm changing it to green and making it smaller."

"That's wonderful," says Reverend Tesla says excitedly. "Now, split it in half. Can you do that?"

Nikola has calmed down now and says, "It's coming apart."

"Wonderful," says Reverend Tesla. "Now, whenever you want to visualize anything, that's how you do it." He pauses and then says, "If something bothers you, visualize something pleasant and it will change your mood."

* * *

Nikola has some friends, but he is often left out because he is more curious and serious about life than they are. One day, a fishing trip is planned because one of the boys has a new fishing line and hook. Nikola gets a glance at it, but they go off without him.

He then searches around and finds some wire, makes a hook with a barb at the end, ties it to a line, and goes off to a different pond by alone. He puts the fishing line in the water, and before long a frog gets caught on the line. Before the day is over, he snares more than a dozen frogs.

He meets his friends coming back from their fishing trip; they have caught nothing. He proudly shows them his bountiful catch.

His friends are important to him, but he is never bored being by himself.

Who invented the radio? (Wireless Transmission of Energy)

Tesla filed his own basic radio patent applications in 1897. They were granted in 1900. Marconi's first patent application in America, filed on November 10, 1900, was turned down. Marconi's revised applications over the next three years were repeatedly rejected because of the priority of Tesla and other inventors.

It wasn't until 1943, a few months after Tesla's death – that The U. S. Supreme Court upheld Tesla's radio patent number 645,576.

Chapter 3

A MOVE TO GOSPIC

A year later the family moves to Gospic, a bustling town six miles west of Smiljan. Nikola, now seven, creates his first experiment in original methods of power production. He takes two thin slivers of wood, as thick as a toothpicks and several times longer, and glues them together in the form of a cross.

Taking a piece of string to act as a driving belt, he slips it over a pulley that has the diameter of a pea and also around the circumference of a much larger but lighter pulley. which is mounted on a thin spindle.

The power for the machine is furnished by sixteen June bugs; four glued to each spindle of the windmill. As the bugs flap their wings, the windmill turns for hours.

Proud of his accomplishment, he checks the windmill and makes minor adjustments to see that it works smoothly.

A few nights later, Nikola is suddenly awakened by the nightmare of Dane's death. A vivid picture of the scene is thrust before his eyes.

"Go away! I'm being tormented!" screams Nikola. The vision shifts to the funeral. "I must think of something pleasant," he says in a quieter tone. He conjures up an image of playing with his cat when he was much younger. They are toying with each other, and he starts laughing as the cat purrs and brushes against him. "Something pleasant. Always something pleasant," he thinks, and the vision fades.

* * *

In the city square near the river, a parade and demonstration is underway to display a new pump which replaces the outdated firefighting bucket brigade. The pump is man-made and is operated by a team of men. Everyone in the city turns out for the event, which is followed by a trip to the riverfront for the pumping demonstration.

The order is given to start the pumping operation that will send a stream of water shooting skyward from the nozzle.

"Start pumping!" shouts the captain.

The men line up on both sides of the pump and are waving the hose up and down, but when the bars are lowered for the water to shoot through, not a drop comes out. A hush falls over the crowd in anticipation. The officials feverishly make adjustments, but after each attempt they have the same disappointing results.

Nikola is trying to see what is going on from the closest possible vantage point.

"Shoo," says the official, "we need room."

"I know what to do, mister," says Nikola. "You keep pumping." He peels off his clothes quickly, dashes to the river, and dives in the water. He swims to the suction hose, finds a kink, and straightens it out so the water can rush through the line.

The men on the shore are unprepared and the water gushes on the officials and part of the crowd. Everyone cheers. Nikola emerges from the water half dressed; he is placed on the shoulders of a couple of firemen to lead the procession around town. Nikola is the Hero of the Day.

* * *

At the young age of seven, he is introduced to a science classroom environment of beakers, measuring devices, experiments with atmospheric pressure, mechanical devices, and gravity. He always sits in the front and is totally absorbed with the experiments.

After learning about chemical changes in the body, he decides to experiment by taking very deep breaths and holding them. By doing so, he discovers he can create a self-induced trance. Soon he is thinking, "I wonder if I can create something that will let me fly."

A few days later he goes to the shed and proceeds to carefully build a box of wood, which has a well-crafted cylinder that fits tightly on one end and on the other side has a right-angle contact. He wants this right-angle contact to produce rotation. If he can get the cylinder to rotate, then he can attach a propeller to the shaft. He straps the box to his body, believing it will contain continuous power through the vacuum box which will then lift him in the air.

He locates a typical air pump and reverses the gears. He keeps trying to pull all of the air out of the cylinder until he aches from the work that is required to keep pumping. He almost gives up, but decides to rest to contemplate the situation.

He starts to breathe deeply to change the chemical balance in his body, and all of a sudden the cylinders starts to turn. Pressure starts to build and he can feel himself being pulled from his position. When the cylinder stops, he primes the pump and starts the proper whirling again.

A few days later, he climbs up to the rooftop of the barn. He opens a parasol and attempts to catch a gust of wind. He manages to catch a small thermal, but it doesn't have enough strength to hold him up and he comes crashing to the ground, hurting himself badly. He spends six weeks in bed recovering.

* * *

Nikola, now thirteen, and some friends are herding cattle along the military frontier of Romania and Yugoslavia (now called Bosnia). Even though it's wintertime, the boys are preparing to sleep out of doors. They're nearing a cornfield.

Nikola suggests sleeping in the cornfield. "It should be safe there for a little while."

The boys are unpacking their bedding and Nikola pulls out a knife. "Put this in the ground and we can tell if the cattle move or if the soldiers are getting closer."

Nikola's friend asks, "How can you tell?"

Nikola puts his ear to the ground. "Listen, the sound travels and the knife vibrates. Keep your ear to the ground while we sleep." He turns to his friend. "Can you hear that?"

"Hear what?" asks his friend.

"The cattle moving around."

"Why, yes. Wow, I wonder how far the sound travels."

Nikola goes to the knife. "Let me see if I can tell. The more the knife vibrates, the closer we are." His friends are fascinated.

Nikola laughs. Let's roll some snow and see how fast we can get a large snowball to go down the hill The bigger they get, the more force they have." He jerks to attention. "Did you hear that?"

"Hear what?" asks his friend.

"That noise. A rustling noise."

They listen, and in unison they respond, "No, we don't hear anything but us."

Nikola looks to the woods. "There's something there."

They go back to rolling some snow, and in a few seconds a deer appears.

"Well, and there is the sound I heard. You didn't hear her?" Nikola asks, surprised. "The earth is a conductor of sound."

With high frequencies, Tesla developed some of the first neon and fluorescent illumination. He took the first x-ray photographs. But these discoveries paled when compared to his discovery of November 1890, when he illuminated a vacuum tube wirelessly – having transmitted energy through air.

Chapter 4

NIKOLA IS VERY SICK

During the 1800s there are no antibiotics or medical facilities like we have today. Childhood illnesses are common, and Nikola gets very sick with cholera while he is visiting at his Aunt Stanka's house. He is due to return home, but his aunt feels he should stay with her a little longer. There is an epidemic of cholera in the area.

Nikola replies, "They're waiting for me at home, and a good dose of Mark Twain always makes me feel better."

He does go home, but he is very ill. A book by Mark Twain is on his bedside table.

His father says, "This cholera is consuming you. I've lost one son; I don't want to lose another."

Nikola responds drowsily, "I understand."

"You must get well, so you can follow my footsteps in the ministry." His father puts his hand on Nikola's forehead and feels his fever. Nikola sinks into an almost unconscious state. He is undernourished and very thin.

A few days later, his father and a doctor are in the bedroom. His mother is with them. Nikola is very weak.

The doctor examines him, and says, "I don't know what more I can do for him. He appears to be giving up the fight."

His father replies sadly, "He has so much to live for. His imagination, his brilliant mind."

"Medically, I've done all I can. The rest is up to him," says the doctor.

Nikola is lying there, weak, with his eyes half-closed. He can barely speak.

His father tries desperately to rouse him and to stir him into a more cheerful mood. In a commanding voice, his father says, "Nikola, you cannot go."

Djourka is holding Nikola's hand. "This is going on much too long."

There is hardly enough energy in Nikola for him to audibly whisper, "I could get well…if you let me study…engineering."

His father bends over intently, seizes him, and says, "You will be an engineer. Do you hear me? You will go to the best technical institute I can find and you will be a great engineer." He pauses, and then says, "You must get well. You will be a *great* engineer if that is what *you* want."

A faint smile curves Nikola's lips and a shine comes into his eyes.

"Thank God! You heard me, Nikola. You will go to an engineering school and become a great engineer. Do you understand me?"

Nikola has no energy to speak, but his smile becomes a little more definite. His mother looks at her husband and Nikola, and sees the faint smile that appears on his lips. She puts her hand on Reverend Tesla's shoulder and looks at both of them very lovingly.

It isn't long afterward that Nikola's fever goes down. He is reading the book written by Mark Twain, and everyone knows he is on the road to recovery.

* * *

Now attending the Polytechnic School at Graz, Nikola is watching Professor Pocschl demonstrating a Gramme machine that can be used either as a dynamo or a motor. It operates on direct current.

"This Gramme machine turns by mechanical power; it will generate electricity, and if supplied with electricity, it can operate as a motor and produce mechanical power," lectures Professor Poeschl.

Nikola is greatly impressed with the demonstration. However, a great deal of sparking is taking place in the commutator. Wincing at the staccato snapping of the spark, he says, "This is not good. It could be dangerous. Can anything be done with that annoying discharge?"

Professor Poeschl replies, "Nothing. We can reduce it, but we can't eliminate it."

"Nonsense," Nikola mumbles.

"It is direct current and we haven't found a way to avoid it," the professor continues. "It seems to be inherent in the nature of the machine. It may be reduced to a great extent, but as long as we use commutators, it will always be present. As long as a magnet has two poles, each of which acts oppositely at the current, we will have to use a commutator to change at the right moment the directions of the current in the rotating armature."

Nikola responds, "That is obvious. The machine is limited by the current used. I am suggesting that we get rid of the commutator entirely by using alternating current."

Nikola's ability at mathematics is phenomenal. He knows the answers as quickly as the professor puts the problems on the board. He figures out the answers mentally and hardly ever writes the problems down.

Back at home, he's meeting with his father.

"Niko, I hate to see you drop out of school."

"Father, I need to get some work experience. There's only so much I can do in the classroom. I'm further advanced than my classmates," says Nikola.

"Where are you planning to go?"

"A lot is happening in Budapest. A telephone company is opening up, and I'm sure I can learn much and contribute much."

"Well, you have my blessings, and we have a little money saved that I can send along with you," says his father.

* * *

In Budapest, Nikola checks in at the Central Telephone Company office. A sign indicates they will open soon.

He's ready to walk away when he notices a dear friend
from school, Anital Szigrati. Nikola waves and catches his
attention.

"What a wonderful surprise! What brings you here?" asks
Nikola.

"I was going to apply for work at the Central Telephone
Company, but I see they're not open yet."

Nikola says, "Let's grab some coffee and get caught up."

As they're sitting at the table, Anital pulls out a deck of
cards and they thoroughly enjoy each other's company.

They both get hired at the Central Telephone Company and
are introduced to the work of Thomas Edison.

After hours, they often take walks in the park close by.
One day, without any warning, Nikola waves his arms in
the air and sways his body, reciting the lines of the German
poet Goethe. Mothers watching their children stare at him.
A few children notice him and watch with fascination.

> *"The glow retreats, done is the day of toil,*
> *It yonder hastes, new fields of life exploring;*
> *Ah, that no wing can lift me from the soil,*
> *Upon its track to follow...soaring!"*

Suddenly, Nikola's animated body snaps into a rigid pose,
as if he has fallen into a trance.

Szigrati speaks to him but gets no answer. "Nikola, can
you hear me?"

Nikola ignores Szigrati's words. His friend is about to
seize him and shake him when…Nikola excitedly blurts
out, "Watch me! Watch me reverse it, if I can get a
magnetic field to rotate! That's all it would take – inducing
rotation in a magnetic field!"

He gazes into the sun. They continue walking, with a
spring in their step. Pointing to a nearby bench, Szigrati
says, "Let's sit and rest for awhile." Nikola is again frozen
in space. He's almost in a trance.

"Nikola, are you ill?" asked Szigrati.

Nikola responds calmly, "It's right here before me. My
alternating current motor; I have solved the problem."
Now excited, he asks, "Don't you see it? See how
smoothly it is running? Now I throw the switch -- I reverse
it. See! It goes just as smooth in the opposite direction.
Watch! I stop it! I start it! There is no sparking. There's
nothing to spark."

Szigrati is confused. "But I see nothing…as you see it."

"You don't understand. It's my alternating current motor
I'm talking about. I solved the problem. It's a rotating
field that does it! My motor will set men free from hard
tasks; it will do the work of the world."

Szigrati starts to shake his head in disbelief. "I can't see it
like you can, but I understand your theory."

Nikola picks up a twig. "Let me show you something else
I've been working on." He squats down and starts drawing
in the dust. "The rotating magnetic field possesses the
property transferring wirelessly through space by means of
its lines of force. This is the basis of an engine which will

22

propel a vehicle. The need for a commutator is eliminated."

Szigrati replies, "You are amazing."

"I know it will work. I see the possibilities." Nikola draws what we know as a "Vertical Take-Off Vehicle" or helicopter. Szigrati is stunned. "You mean a flying machine!"

"Well, yes, one that hovers and can land in a small space. The rotors lift the craft with very little energy pull."

They get up to walk. "We just don't have the knowledge to build something like that," says Szigrati.

Nikola replies, "I'm working on the details. The electrical charges need to rotate the blades. They are the key to the whole idea. I've got a working model I've been tinkering with. The answer to progress is **magnetics** and **energy**."

They continue walking.

"I have an offer to work in France at the Consolidated Edison Company. I'll be working on dynamos, and motors, and installing lighting systems under the Edison patents."

"I'll miss you, Nikola."

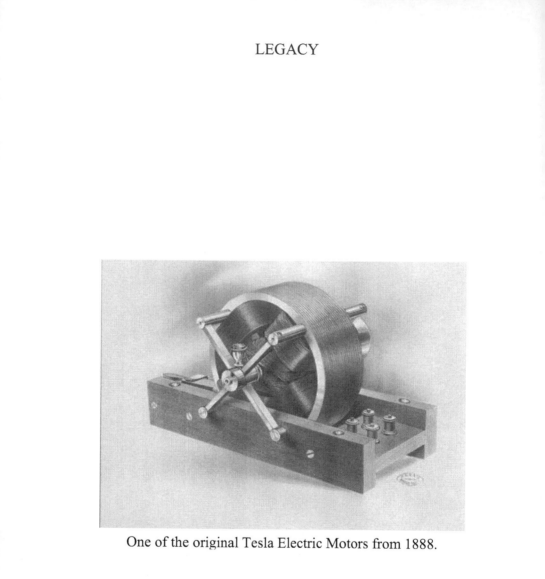

One of the original Tesla Electric Motors from 1888.

Chapter 5

WORKING

Dr. Cunningham is in charge of the Continental Edison Company in Paris. Nikola is in his office discussing alternating current to solve some of the electrical problems.

Nikola says, "The company needs to work on alternating current. It is the wave of the future."

Dr. Cunningham responds, "I can't speak or override Edison's patents. All I can suggest is that you form your own company."

"I'm not interested in building my own business. There's much we can do here."

Dr. Cunningham shrugs and says, "I'm limited; my hands are tied. However, there are some installations in France and Germany that need your expertise. The powerhouses are having trouble carrying the load. Can you handle the problem?"

"Sure, and I speak French and German fluently."

Nikola travels to the various factories, investigates the different problems, and makes notations. He talks with the foremen and checks the transmission lines. He returns to

Dr. Cunningham's office. "I suggest you improve the dynamos. They're hindering your capacity. I also suggest we design some automatic regulators. That should solve the problem at all the facilities."

"Tesla, would you like to work in the machine shop in Strasbourg to help fix a problem?" asks Dr. Cunningham. "We'll give you extra pay."

Weeks later, Nikola has a machinist apron over his suit and, is polishing a piece of equipment to an exact dimension. Then he starts assembling a dynamo to generate the two-phase alternating current. He starts up the power generator and thinks quietly to himself, "If I close the switch and if the motor turns, my theory is correct."

He shuffles parts around, rechecks his dynamo, closes the switch, closes his eyes for a moment, and looks up to the ceiling. Instantly the armature turns, building up to full speed in a flash, and continues to operate in complete silence. He closes the reversing switch, and the armature quickly stops and starts turning in the opposite direction. Very excited, Nikola says to himself, "I've done it. I've done it! My theory is right."

After a few weeks, he returns to Paris. He enters Dr. Cunningham's office and attempts to collect the extra compensation he was promised. "I'm over the production department," Dr. Cunningham says. "I have no authority over your compensation. Check with the accounting department."

After being sent from one office to another, Nikola returns to Dr. Cunningham's office. He is angry. "I resign. I'm not renewing my offer to stay. I must move on."

Dr. Cunningham realizes how valuable Nikola is and asks, "Do you want to go to America to meet Mr. Edison, to see if you can work together?"

Nikola's mood changes and he sees this as an opportunity. "Is this a job offer?"

"No, all I can do is write a Letter of Introduction."

Nikola nods his head and says, "Sure, I'll give it a try."

* * *

Nikola is at the train station. He is wearing white gloves and a bowler hat, his usual red and black tie, and a high-button shirt. He is always meticulously dressed everywhere he goes or works. However, he can't find his baggage, and his wallet containing his steamship ticket and his money is missing. He finds some coins in his pocket. He runs alongside the train and jumps on board.

The conductor sees him. "Where is your fare?"

"I lost my steamship ticket and my train ticket."

"If no one claims your space, you can board. Wait here until everyone checks in."

At the steamship office, they check the records and find he purchased a ticket. The trip is uncomfortable without his baggage. As the steamship is pulling into New York Harbor, workmen are on the scaffolding around the Statue of Liberty. The excitement of the passengers coming to America and the activity level in the harbor is overwhelming. A gentle breeze is whipping through Nikola's hair and he has a far-off look in his eyes.

As he approaches the immigration officer, he empties his pockets. He has four cents, a book of his poems, a couple of technical articles he wrote, his design for the flying machine, his introduction letter to Thomas Edison, and the address of a friend he is to stay with.

The immigration officer is impressed. "Looks like you've got a lot of work ahead of you."

Nikola responds, "I'll be fine."

The immigration officer stamps his paperwork and says, "Good luck."

It is mid-day in New York. Nikola starts walking to the address of his friend, checks the address and the map, and counts his steps, avoiding the cracks in the sidewalk as he walks. He passes a shop, peers in the window, and sees a man working on a familiar electrical machine. He is having difficulty. Nikola opens the door and speaks as the man is about to give up. "Looks like you have a problem here. Let me do it. I can make it operate."

The man steps aside gladly. Nikola snatches a wrench from the toolbox and matches it to a half-inch nut and twists. He unscrews the nuts and bolts that hold the casing together and lifts it apart, being assisted by a young man in the shop. Together they open the casing and expose the armature.

"This is the problem," says Nikola.

He points to a sliver of copper that has come loose from the coil and has fallen between the armature and the casing. "Let me remove it. There. The metal hasn't been badly scored. Let me fix the wire coil, and I'll have it back together in less than ten minutes."

The shop owner is amazed. "I need someone who understands these foreign machines. Do you want a job?"

"No thanks, tomorrow I'm to meet someone who hopefully will have a job for me."

The shop owner hands Nikola a twenty-dollar bill. "Your efforts are worth more than this."

"Thanks, this will come in handy."

Nikola is elated. He now has money for food and incidentals.

* * *

The next day, Nikola arrives at Mr. Edison's prestigious office with his bowler hat in his hand. Nellie, his secretary, opens Mr. Edison's door and announces Nikola's arrival. "Mr. Tesla has a Letter of Introduction for you from Mr. Batchelor in Paris."

Thomas Edison responds, "I'm with the Johnsons. Can you have him come back tomorrow?"

Robert Johnson is the editor of *Century* magazine, which covers the arts and sciences. He is very popular with the artistic and scientific notables of the time. His attractive wife, Katherine, is with him.

LEGACY

Robert Johnson interjects, "Tom, he's here, our conversation can wait. Let him in. He's the gentleman from Serbia and I'd love to meet him."

Edison nods to Nellie and says to Robert Johnson, "Okay, I'd like you to meet him." Nellie brings him into the inner office.

This towering, lanky, six-foot-three-inch man comes in and hands the papers to Edison. Edison is very cordial. "I've heard much about you. Welcome to America." Edison extends his hand, but Nikola does not shake it. Instead, he gives a slight bow. Edison notices, but doesn't say anything.

In a very businesslike way, Nikola says, "I'm very glad to be here, and I'm looking forward to getting to work as quickly as possible."

Edison introduces him to the Johnsons. Robert Johnson smiles and says, "Very pleased to meet you. You must come to our house this Saturday. We're having a gathering of many friends."

"I appreciate the invitation. I'll be there." Edison extends his hand, but Nikola just nods. The Johnsons noticed this and look at him with curiosity.

Katherine walks up to him. "We will look forward to seeing you Saturday night. Tom will give you directions."

Edison walks around his desk. "Report to my lab at this address tomorrow morning. The foreman will be expecting you. We'll discuss compensation then."

Nikola, holding his hat, nods and walks toward the door.

The Life of Nikola Tesla

* * *

That Saturday night, many people are milling around at the Johnsons' house. Katherine introduces Nikola to Samuel Clemens (who writes as Mark Twain).

Nikola asks, "Do we call you Samuel or Mark?"

Samuel Clemens laughs. "I answer to both."

"I've been a fan of yours for as long as I can remember. Please accept my debt of gratitude that my very life, my will to live, was rescued from oblivion by your books. That is true, sir."

Clemens responds, "This is the most joyous news of my life, sir. To think those books I wrote influenced such a towering figure of a man. I am humbled, Mr. Tesla, truly humbled."

"As I am humbled before you, sir," Nikola says.

"Welcome to the clan," says Samuel Clemens. They both nod and smile.

Katherine continues with the introductions, "John Muir, Ann Morgan."

Nikola nods with his hands in his pockets. "Pleased to meet you. Are you related to
J. P. Morgan?"

Ann replies, "Yes, he's my father. His office seems to be the crossroads of the world."

Nikola laughs, "Maybe I'll be one of his visitors soon."

Katherine continues with the introductions, "Rudyard Kipling, Nathaniel Hawthorne."

"My goodness," says Nikola, "the literary world is well represented."

"George Westinghouse."

"Another inventor. What a pleasure!"

"Antonin Dvorak." Katherine turns directly to the composer. "Please play some passages from your new composition."

Dvorak responds, "Only with a little coaxing." He sits down at the piano, does a run on the keyboard, and then plays portions of his *"New World Symphony."* Some of the guests surround the piano while others remain sitting or standing where they are, totally absorbed.

* * *

A few weeks later, Nikola is working in Edison's laboratory with other staff members on a routine electrical problem. Edison arrives and seems fairly pleased with his work.

"How is it going?" asks Edison.

"My thinking is if you utilized a polyphase system with alternating current to use in the power and lighting system, it will be more efficient and less costly."

Edison quickly responds, "I'm not interested in alternating current. There is no future to it and anyone dabbling in the field is wasting his time. Besides, it's a deadly current; direct current is safe. People like it and it's all we use here."

Nikola realizes he had better not say anymore; however, he knows he won't yield.

"We are installing an electric-light plant on the steamship *Oregon*. It's a passenger ship and we're having unpredictable delays. Would you like to tackle the problem?"

Nikola shows interest, saying, "I'd love to help. What seems to be the problem?"

"It seems impossible to remove the old dynamos and install new ones, so we're repairing what's there. Do you want to go to the ship to see what needs to be done?"

Nikola smiles. "I appreciate the challenge."

A few days later, he has a crew working with him through the night. He looks refreshed; the crew looks exhausted.

"I think we did it, and a job well done. It's been a long night, thanks for all your help. Why don't you guys get some sleep? I'll head over to Edison's lab."

Walking back to the shop at 5:00 a.m., he runs into Edison and a group of men just arriving. "Well," says Edison, "looks like much is happening at the wee hours of the morning."

Nikola is proud. "We're all up late…or early. Both machines are operating."

Later that day Nikola is in Edison's office. Edison is very happy. "I have had many hard-working employees, but you take the cake."

"Thank you, I love my work."

Edison seems quite excited. "We talked about our dynamos. I need increased output and efficiency with them. Can you help me? There's fifty thousand dollars in it for you if you can."

"I know I can. Can you offer me some staff?"

"Pick who you need," Edison says willingly.

Four months later, Nikola delivers all the equipment running efficiently. Edison says, "You kept your promise, so I'm offering you a ten dollar a week raise."

Nikola is stunned. "Ten dollars per week! What happened to the fifty thousand you mentioned?"

"Oh, that was just a figure of speech," says Edison.

Nikola looks around at the expensive furnishings, then looks at Edison. He is angry. "Consider this my resignation." He picks up his hat and walks out.

Chapter 6

TESLA AND WESTINGHOUSE

Months later, in the New York streets, while digging in a ditch, Nikola Tesla is leaning on a shovel and talking to a foreman. He is wearing a vest and a red and black tie, but no jacket or hat. A number of other people are also digging the same ditch.

The foreman is saying, "We're both here not by financial choice. With your talent, this is a crime against humanity. I know someone at Western Union Telegraph Company. If you can do with electricity what you were telling me, maybe he'll be interested in your inventions."

"I would appreciate meeting him very much. I'd better get back to work or we'll never finish this job."

"Let's see if we can all meet next week," his foreman says.

"The sooner the better," responds Nikola.

A few days later, they are all in A. K. Brown's office at The Western Union Telegraph Company. Mr. Brown speaks. "We're very impressed with what you've accomplished. This alternating current, will it work with telegraphy?"

"Of course," Nikola replies. "It will affect communication, transportation, and utilities. There are many other uses that I also have in mind."

Quite interested, A. K. Brown says, "I'll put together a few investors and we'll help you set up shop. Half a million dollars is a lot of money, but I think it will be a very good investment."

"Mr. Brown, I can't thank you enough. This is a wonderful opportunity, and I'm sure you'll be proud of being part of my company."

Mr. Brown extends his hand, and Nikola gets up and politely bows.

In 1887, The Tesla Electric Company is established in Rahway, New Jersey, fairly close to Edison's laboratory. Many pieces of equipment are neatly aligned on workbenches, such as cathode tubes, Tesla coils, etc. George Westinghouse, the founder of the Westinghouse Corporation, is very friendly with Nikola Tesla and is visiting him.

Nikola tells him, "I've just submitted the patents for the automatic control system, the dynamos, and the motor. Next month I should be ready for the transformer patent."

"I'll give you one million in cash for the alternating currents patent, plus royalties," offers George Westinghouse.

"George, if you'll make the royalty one dollar per volt sold, I will accept the offer."

"You'll have a check in a few days." George Westinghouse is intrigued with all the apparatus. "Sure looks like you've got something the world can appreciate."

A few months later, the Johnsons and George Westinghouse are in the judge's chambers while Nikola is receiving his citizenship papers.

The judge says, "We proudly welcome you as one of our citizens."

"I am proud to be an American citizen, and hope the American people will be proud to have me."

* * *

It is 1893. Thomas Edison is reading *The Scientific News* and comes across the information that Nikola Tesla made an agreement with Westinghouse on the alternating current system for the Chicago World Fair. He throws the magazine down on the floor and jumps up angrily. "Nellie! Nellie! Come here at once!"

Nellie runs in and sees with relief that Edison is okay. "What is the matter?" She sees the magazine on the floor and calmly picks it up.

"That upstart Tesla has signed an agreement with Westinghouse. He can't get away with that. Did you know accidents caused by alternating currents could be fatal?"

Nellie jumps out of the way as Edison angrily paces back and forth. He shoves a pen and paper at Nellie. "Take a note. No, write a press release. 'Accidents caused by alternating currents could be avoided by utilizing the direct current system. The public must be alerted.' I must contact Pupin and Marconi and oppose Tesla. The public doesn't need all this confusion. The direct current will serve their needs."

George Westinghouse is visiting Nikola at his laboratory. Nikola is sitting down, with his legs on his desk, and reading the Niagara Commission Report. "The Niagara Commission wants to pay three-thousand dollars for the most practical plan to set up a direct current generating plant."

Westinghouse responds, "Very clever. They can receive a hundred-thousand dollars of information for three-thousand dollars. Let's not respond, and when we do, it will be with an alternating current proposal that will give Edison a run for his money."

Nikola laughs. "I wonder if Edison will respond. Here, let me show you this." He gets up, washes his hands, and then does an electrical and magnetic demonstration that fascinates George Westinghouse.

"Absolutely fascinating," says Westinghouse. "What do you see as its application?"

"I'll probably use it for wireless transmission for now. It could have many applications."

Westinghouse changes the subject. "I think in all the excitement I forgot to tell you I got the contract for installing all the power and lighting equipment for the Chicago World Fair. We're going to use alternating current."

"Well, by golly, that is great news!" says Nikola, getting excited.

People are walking around at the Chicago World Fair, some briskly, some strolling. Various pavilions are set up. Some of the buildings have signs: Agriculture, Manufacturing, and Electricity. It is a very important worldwide exposition.

In the Electricity Pavilion, people are gathered in total fascination. There is a display of the early stages of robotics being demonstrated. The Tesla coil is hooked to devices generating electricity, which is then used for creating activity, including the lighting of fluorescent tubes. Displays of the Westinghouse Electric Polyphase System and Edison Electric Bulb are also present. People are pushing buttons and lifting switches, enjoying the wonders of modern science.

* * *

J. P. Morgan, a powerful financier who is backing Edison, is talking to his assistant in his beautifully decorated office. "Tesla is making quite a name for himself, both in the technical journals and the press. I keep reading about the competition between Tesla and Edison. I need to acquire the patents so we can centralize this electricity squabble."

His assistant responds, "He is always in need of money; I'm sure you'll be seeing him in the not-too-distant future."

"Look how efficient the nation has become with the consolidation of the railroads, the steel mills, and the oil companies," says Morgan.

"Yes," says his assistant, "it is for the well-being of the nation."

"The world," responds Morgan.

About a year later, J. P. Morgan is having a meeting with one of his financial people, Jason Gray. His rivalry with Ned Harriman of the railroads and George Westinghouse of electricity is coming to a head. He is pointing to a wall map. "Now that we own the Chicago Line, we've control of the north. Harriman just has control of Southern Pacific now. If I buy more trunks, we can squeeze him out."

Gray says, "That ought to put Wall Street in a buzz."

"Speaking of Wall Street, I hear Westinghouse is over-extended. Let's put some selling pressure on the stock. We don't want to go in with Westinghouse. Edison won't stand for that."

Shortly thereafter, George Westinghouse is standing near the doorway of the lab at his company, holding his hat and looking quite depressed. Nikola is tinkering and looks up. "Come in. This isn't like you," he says,

"With the rumors on Wall Street, my stock has taken a dive. I'm trying to arrange a merger, and the financial advisors said I need to get rid of the royalty contract with you or the merger won't go through. It is a large liability on the company. Can we reduce it to fifty cents a volt?"

Nikola walks over to his safe, opens it, and pulls out the note. He tears it in half. "Consider the contract void. We've been friends for too long to have money come between us. We've done many good things together and will continue to do so. Let's both move on with our lives."

"Do you realize this contract has been in effect for four years and you haven't claimed any of your royalties?" asks Westinghouse.

"I haven't needed the money. Without the contract you will save your company and retain control. You will proceed with your plans to give my polyphase system to the world."

Clearing his throat, Westinghouse says, "I believe your polyphase system is the greatest discovery in the field of electricity. I will continue my efforts to put the country on alternating current."

"Now, I think we both have much to do," says Nikola. "Oh, by the way, look at this." They walk over to the bench with some of the inventions on it. "Come, let me show you what I'm doing with the wireless transmission. This should handle broadcasting intelligence globally and has interplanetary potential."

Westinghouse says, "You've got to take a rest. You've been going day and night for months. Do you sleep at all?"

"Very little, so much to do. Let me show you my Telautomata." (This is the forerunner of the robot.) Nikola maneuvers it by remote control. "It will be capable of acting as if possessed of its own intelligence."

"Nikola, you're treading on hallowed ground," says Westinghouse.

They walk toward the door. Nikola says, "We all must have an ideal to be self-sufficient, govern our conduct, and ensure contentment. Unlimited energy is a necessary ingredient."

LEGACY

Westinghouse humbly says, "Thank you so much. You are incredible." He nervously turns his hat in his hand and walks out.

* * *

Nikola Tesla has just completed a major presentation to an international conference of businessmen, scientists, and the press. He has demonstrated how much lighter AC current is over DC current when a switch is pulled. The audience was fascinated and the demonstration was very successful.

As he leaves the building, he gets a strong vision that his mother is dying. He turns to his colleague. "I must divert my plans. My mother is very ill. I must leave for Serbia tomorrow. Please apologize for my absence. I've got to run and make arrangements."

"How do you know?" asks his colleague, who is stunned. "If we need to reach you, what do we do?"

"I can't believe anything would be that urgent, but send a message to the following address. She doesn't have a phone."

Traveling is slow and he reaches his mother's side just as she is dying. Friends and family are in the room.

Mrs. Tesla asks, "How did you know?"

Nikola answers, "I had a vision, like information that is given to me many times. It happens frequently."

"Nikola, we hear great things about you. We are all so proud." She holds his hand, and he realizes this is the first time he has allowed anyone to hold his hand. He looks at

42

her lovingly. "I'm sorry I haven't visited. I'm so involved in my work."

"And the world will be a better place," says Mrs. Tesla.

Nikola stays a few days to help take care of matters. He wanders out into the beautiful countryside and walks through the cornfields. He remembers his brother's death when he was thrown from a horse. He walks around the familiar countryside with a nostalgic look.

Nikola is back in his laboratory when he receives a call from George Westinghouse.

Westinghouse is very excited. "The war of the currents is won. We were awarded the contract at Niagara to build the first two generators."

"Well, that is good news. Am I needed in New York?"

"Immediately," says Westinghouse.

A few months later there is a gathering at the Johnsons' house. Mark Twain, John Muir, and Ned Harriman, along with Nikola Tesla, are enjoying each other's company.

Robert Johnson brings John Muir to him. "Nikola, I'd like to introduce you to John Muir. We've had some excellent articles on nature written by him in our magazine lately."

"Pleased to meet you. I've read with much interest your ideas on conservation. My alternating current will cut down the use of fossil fuel."

John Muir responds, "But you're diverting some of the Niagara water upstream, which is only the beginning of destroying the wonders of nature."

Harriman interrupts, "I share your concern, John. But remember, you're talking to a railroad man. We had to cut down forests for the right-of-way, and it's always gut-wrenching to weigh man's needs for progress against nature's environment."

Nikola is enjoying the conversation. "We need the visions of John Muir as we need the stories of Mark Twain and a better way of life for mankind. Electricity will not only free man from hard labor, it will heal and increase his energy. There is still so much to learn, even from simple things like crystals that have an energy all their own. Come, let's enjoy the chamber music."

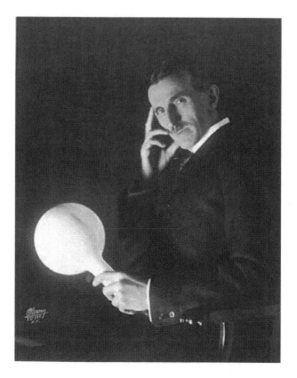

Chapter 7

DISASTER STRIKES

It is early dawn and a frantic knock is heard on the door.
Nikola is feeding the pigeons he keeps in his apartment.
He puts down the bird seed and hurries to answer the door.
He opens it with great concern because he gets very few
visitors, and this is unusually early in the morning.

"Czito, what brings you here at this hour?"

Czito is frantic. "The laboratory is burning down. All the
equipment...all the work...all the notes." He's now
sobbing.

"Come in, come in, and let me get my things."

A major fire burns the laboratory. Nikola watches as the
notes, equipment, and furniture are consumed. The firemen
are struggling to contain it, but without much success. He
places his hand on his forehead and, then wanders away,
counting his steps. He later walks through the rubble with
his hands in his pockets. "How could this have started?"

About a week later, Katherine says to Robert Johnson, "We
must help him. This was his life and the hope of the
world."

Robert asks, "Where do we begin?"

In his apartment, Nikola is reading a letter from Katherine. "Perhaps we might help you. We have so much sympathy to give." He throws the letter away. There's a knock at the door. A Mr. Adams is acknowledged. Nikola gestures toward a chair.

"Well, Mr. Tesla, have you considered the Cataract Company offer?"

"Yes, Mr. Adams."

"Have you reached a conclusion?"

"Yes, I have."

"Very good, what is it?"

"Tell your associate, Mr. Morgan, I have the highest respect for him."

"I see. Is that all?"

"Tell him I have a great respect for him and for the companies he has chosen to represent. Especially his own company, which I regard with esteem."

"I see. Is that all?"

"I guess you know what I am leading to, Mr. Adams."

"Please tell me."

"I am grateful for the forty-thousand-dollar advance. I shall endeavor to make good use of the money, but as for the greater offer, I have decided to decline."

"Is that your final word on the offer?"

"Yes, it is, Mr. Adams."

Mr. Adams says, "Then I guess this discussion is finished."

"Yes, it seems to be concluded."

Mr. Adams stands. "Then I guess I have no further business here."

Nikola responds, "It seems not."

Mr. Adams heads for the door. "Goodbye, Mr. Tesla."

"Goodbye, sir."

Later, the Johnsons are in the neighborhood near his hotel and find him feeding the pigeons. Katherine says, "Come, let's get something to eat. We'll work something out."

"My life's work has gone up in smoke."

Robert responds, "Your mind has the ability to re-create."

They slowly walk together, sharing the despair and the hope. Nikola is counting his steps between conversations. This is one of his many quirks.

"Has anyone heard from Edison? His laboratory is down the street," asks Robert Johnson.

"Nothing from him," says Tesla.

A month later at the Johnsons' house, Katherine is reading letters received for Nikola. "The House of Morgan is offering you backing to rebuild the laboratory."

Nikola responds, "They'll end up owning everything."

"What about the letter from Edward Dean Adams? He was instrumental in funding the Niagara project."

"I'd rather go with him. That seems more to my liking. It's less money, but I have more control over my laboratory."

Katherine says softly, "Nikki, we want to make sure you do what's best for you. What else can I do to help?"

Nikola responds, "You already have. Thanks so much."

* * *

At the Westinghouse Pittsburgh plant, the workers recognize Nikola and look up from their work to greet him with awe and respect. As he enters Westinghouse's modest office, Nikola sees that his inventions are on display, including the Tesla coil.

George Westinghouse is beaming. "Demand and production have increased substantially for your motors, but we just don't have the available resources to tackle the power plants."

"We both know they're obsolete," says Nikola. "But remember, the Europeans sent Alternating Current (AC) 130 miles. We need that kind of capability here."

"Damn financial problems; nuisance lawsuits from Morgan just to keep the financial pressure on, and now Steinmetz is competing using your inventions."

Feeling annoyed, Nikola says, "Use your vision. Don't get bogged down with daily problems. We'll solve them. You know my system must prevail. With Niagara working smoothly, the factories in the area are now experiencing increased production and we're benefiting from that."

George Westinghouse says, "The truth is, some of these patents will be in the public domain in twelve years."

"All the more reason to move forward. The race is on. Here, hand me some papers -- I've got a vision for the new power generators."

Westinghouse hands him a paper and watches him quickly sketch the mechanism. "How do you know the design will work?"

"I'm turning it over in my mind and envisioning all possibilities. This, with the Westinghouse logo, will get those power plants running more efficiently for many years to come."

Interior of Power House No.1 of the Niagara Falls
Power Company (1895-1899).

The first wireless transmission experiments were
performed at this Experimental Station at Colorado
Springs (1899-1900).

Chapter 8

WORLDWIDE RECOGNITION

In 1889, Tesla is riding in a horse-drawn carriage in Paris, and passes the Eiffel Tower as it is being erected. He is there to make a major presentation to the scientific world.

Inside the Universal Exposition Building, the audience is riveted while watching his spectacular display of electrical charges.

Nikola tells the audience, "There is no subject more captivating, more worthy of study, than nature. To understand this mechanism, to discover the forces which are active, and the laws which govern them, is the highest aim of the intellect of man."

Every chair in the auditorium is occupied. Absolute silence prevails. Everyone is focused on Nikola. "Nature has stored up in the universe infinite energy. To capture the unseen resources of nature around us, I will display the power of the unseen energy available to those who have discovered its mysteries."

Nikola turns on a few switches and sparks fly around him. He proceeds with confidence. The audience applauds wildly.

"The spark of an induction coil, the glow of an incandescent lamp. The manifestations of the mechanical forces of current and magnets are no longer beyond our grasp." The audience is spellbound.

"Here is a simple glass tube from which the air has been partially exhausted. I take hold of it; I bring my body in contact with a wire conveying *alternating currents of high potential*, and the tube in my hand is brilliantly lit." He moves the tube.

"In whatever position I may put it, wherever I move in space, as far as I can reach, its soft, pleasing light persists with undiminished brightness."

As the tube he holds begins to glow, he is demonstrating the safety of alternating current. The Edison agent rises and hurries from the hall. George Westinghouse, in the front row, leans forward and is all smiles. The audience applauds wildly again. Nikola continues by walking over to another object. "This is a motor that runs on only one wire, the return circuit occurring wirelessly in space. This knowledge will allow motors to run without any wires at all. There is energy in space, free for the taking."

In the 1890s, Nikola's assistant, George Scherff, is working with lead shields. In the laboratory, Nikola explains to Scherff, "This equipment will photograph the insides of an object. It uses high-energy radio frequencies. Come, let's try a few experiments."

Nikola washes his hands and then demonstrates x-ray techniques. "This is potentially very dangerous. Lead shields must be used. I understand Edison damaged his eyes from x-rays."

Scherff asks, "What is your input?"

"I use high-energy fields, compared to ultra-violet or visible rays."

"What do you envision the end product to be?"

Nikola quickly responds, "Medical purposes, but both people and equipment can be x-rayed."

* * *

A stack of fresh white linen napkins are beside Nikola's plate at a café. By the look in his eye, he appears seriously troubled. A reporter is sitting across from him. They are drinking coffee, and Nikola is being interviewed.

"I'm afraid that you won't find me a pleasant companion tonight. The fact is, I almost killed myself."

The reporter asks, "What happened?"

The waitress brings the meal. Nikola starts to measure the cubic content of the food. He eats a few bites and takes the top napkin off the stack. He wipes his mouth gently and then crumples it. "I got a shock of nearly 3.5 million volts. The sparks jumped three feet through the air and struck me here, on the right shoulder. I tell you, it made me feel dizzy. If my assistant hadn't turned off the current instantly, it would have been the end of me."

The reporter asks, "How far can sparks travel?"

"I have frequently had sparks from my high-tension machine jump the width or length of the laboratory, some thirty to forty feet."

He takes a bite, picks up another napkin, wipes his mouth, and then crumples it. He sits silently for a moment, reflecting. "As ideas go chasing through my brain, I hurry as fast as I can to develop these ideas, only to find someone else is working on them."

"When do you find out?" asks the reporter.

"Sometimes in the trade notices, or patent applications, sometimes through a colleague, and it is indeed a heartache." He continues to eat, pulling another napkin off the stack.

The reporter asks, "Do you believe in marriage for persons with artistic temperaments?"

He answers, "For an artist, yes; for a musician, yes; for a writer, yes; but for an inventor, no. The first three gain inspiration from a woman's love, but an inventor has so intense a nature that his devotion would be directed to others rather than his work. It's a pity, too, for sometimes we feel so lonely."

Chapter 9

THE JOHNSONS' HOUSE PARTY

Music is playing in the background. Nikola is talking to Ann Morgan on an intellectual level when Katherine Johnson comes up. Katherine asks, "What are you up to lately?"

"I'm hoping to file my patent on wireless transmission soon, and George and I are working on the teleautomatic principle. I hope to have models set up within the next few months. Remote control activity could be a big boost not only to the housewife, but to the military. We never seem to have enough money for what we're trying to accomplish and the long, hard hours catch all our attention."

Ann says, "Maybe Daddy can help you out."

"I appreciate the suggestion, but not yet. I've got to try to finish what we're doing with our available resources."

Coyly, Ann says, "Just let me know when you want to meet Daddy. Are you going to see Dvorak's *New World Symphony* next week?"

Nikola responds, "I haven't given it a thought."

"Well, I just happen to have front-row seats. Can I convince you to take me?"

"It's been an awful long time since I've found the time to enjoy such an evening. I'd be delighted."

Mark Twain walks up. "Nikola, we need to sit and have a chess game one of these days. Too much time in the lab can dull the senses."

Nikola laughs. "It's not my senses, it's my personality."

They all laugh together.

Mark Twain remarks, "Somewhere out in the universe I heard you and Einstein were working on some far-out experiments."

"Don't know how the word got out, but we're curious about the relationship of time and space," responds Nikola. "So much of my attention has hit competition that my ideas are being stolen. I will not give up my concepts of power transmission and broadcasting."

Twain jokingly says, "Someone needs to get the word out. The printed page takes so long. It's never easy to be ahead of one's time."

"You know Marconi won the Nobel Prize in Physics for his separate but parallel development of the wireless telegraph," says Nikola with disappointment, "using my patents."

Twain is very understanding. "You can only do so much. Quit fretting – the world is realizing what you have done;

they just don't realize the hardships we all go through to make things happen."

"Humanity has not sufficiently advanced to be willingly led. Maybe in our present world, at best, revolutionary ideas are hampered and ill-treated to be put through the test of time and bitter trials and tribulations," says Nikola wistfully.

Twain says, "It lends itself to being attacked and ridiculed, but we learn to have thick skins. We writers have similar problems."

"Only to emerge all the more triumphantly from the struggle," says Nikola. "The strength of a man shows itself in adversity. Unfortunately, adversity also reveals weakness."

Robert Johnson joins the group. "What's this I hear about you going to Long Island?"

"Didn't I tell you?" responds Nikola.

"No, I haven't seen you in ages."

"Well, I may have the opportunity later this year to set up an experimental station. I've got some financial backing, but I have to finish a few things I've got going here, and I need at least another hundred-thousand dollars."

Robert Johnson responds quickly, "If there's anything to say, write an article for the magazine. It's been awhile since my readers have heard from you."

"I've got to contact H. Stanford White to do the architectural work. I want to have it large enough to transmit wireless to England. Our goal is to develop a worldwide wireless system well ahead of Marconi, and to learn how to send energy abundantly and cheaply without wires to the ends of the earth." Nikola pauses for a second. "I am funded for a laboratory in Colorado Springs, which I'll start first."

Daily lightning storms in Colorado Springs are of great magnitude and intensity. Nikola makes a very detailed study of the natural lightning, learning a great deal about the various kinds of discharges.

During one of the lightning storms he is in the lab with George Scherff, his other assistant. They see lightning strike ten miles away. Making a quick computation, Tesla says, "Watch, we'll be hit in 48.5 seconds."

In exactly 48.5 seconds, a tidal wave of air strikes a terrific blow to the building, knocking out all the windows on one side. A door is demolished and other parts of the interior are also damaged.

"I estimate that the concussion was about equal to twelve tons of dynamite ignited ten miles away. Let's start cleaning up. We have work to do. We will prove the earth is an electrically charged body."

He and Scherff go out to read some instruments. Nikola, interpreting some data, says, "Just as I predicted. We're predicting the force of lightning."

Later that week, the night sky explodes with sound and color. The earth seems alive and the crash of thunder from the spark gap can be heard for miles. Nikola and Scherff wear cotton in their ears as they work nightly amid the thunder and lightning. Fireballs are skitting across the floor.

"Look at those fireballs," says Nikola. "I wonder what causes them." Inside the laboratory, he says to George Scherff, "When I give you the word, you close the switch for one second – no longer." Nikola takes a position near the door of the laboratory where he can view the giant coil in the center of the great barn-like room.

"Now!"

George Scherff jams home the switch and quickly pulls it out. In that brief interval, the secondary coil is crowned with a mass of hair-like electrical fire; there is a crackling sound in various parts of the room and a sharp snap overhead.

"Fine," says Nikola, "the experiment is working beautifully. We'll try it again in exactly the same way. Now!"

The electrical discharges get brighter with a blue hue and the sound is becoming thunderous. Nikola is mesmerized with the longer and wider bolts of lightning he is creating. After a fantastic lightning display and ear-shattering noise, everything comes to a halt.

"George!, George, why did you do that?" George points to the switch. It is still closed. He then points to the measuring instruments. Everything is zero. The incoming wires carrying power to the laboratory are dead. "George, call the power company quickly. They must not do that. They cut off my power." The telephone call is put through.

"This is Nikola Tesla. You have cut off my power. You must give it back to me immediately."

The employee at the power company answers gruffly, "Cut off your power, nothing. You threw a short circuit and cut out power to the whole city. No one has power."

The next day, Nikola goes to the power company. "I'll pay the cost of an extra-special rush job if you'll let my workers handle everything." He has it all fixed within a week.

A small party is held at the mayor's office. The mayor makes a toast. "I'd like to toast Mr. Tesla, whose interesting edifice adorns the outskirts of our city. If it produces the results which he expects, then we shall certainly be put on the map as the birthplace of a new era in the history of electricity."

Late one night, the elderly carpenter, Dozier, who works for Nikola, hears a sudden strange rhythmic sound that breaks through the silence. It is coming over the radio receiver.

Nikola says, "Do you hear that?"

"Sure do," says Dozier. "Where is it coming from?"

"The radio transmitter." Nikola walks outside to look at the sky. "I think we have interplanetary communication." Thrilled and awestruck, he can only sit and listen. "I wonder if I can return the signal. There must be a way."

Chapter 10

WARDENCLYFFE BROADCASTING
LONG ISLAND, NEW YORK

H. Stanford White and Nikola Tesla proceed to a drafting table where Nikola holds up various blueprint views of the tower.

"We have to think BIG, Stanford!"

White examines the plans, then gazes out the window. "Now, Nikki, this is already much larger than we planned, and you need to build the receiver in England, too. You won't have the funds."

"Money is no problem. J. P. Morgan offered to back me up."

White is concerned. "I'm only cautioning you, hopeless as that may seem, but why this big change in plans?"

Nikola responds angrily, "Treachery, that's why! It's that parasite Marconi. He has written articles condemning my apparatus and now I see he's illegally using my equipment." Nikola slaps a magazine article down. He points to a circled article. "...Syntonic Wireless Telegraphy by Guglielmo Marconi. I first constructed an arrangement which includes what may be called a Tesla coil."

White is shocked. "My God, you're right. Well, I hope he remembers to get royalties to you."

"Knowing him, I doubt it. Read on, there's worse."

White continues, "The idea of using a Tesla coil to produce oscillations is not new. It was tried in 1898, and suggested by a patent."

Nikola is furious. "Not new is right! The pinhead!, THAT is my patent!"

White agrees with Nikola. "He's even advertising his piracy in print. It's incredible!"

Nikola is getting firmer in his vision. "This tower has got to be much bigger. You must double the height."

"Double?"

"Yes, double. Don't you see? When our tower is complete, it will send not just more impulses to England, but light, pictures, and power to Europe, and to the whole world!"

Nikola's gaze causes White to sit down at the table and begin immediately to alter the scale of the blueprints. White says, "I'd better tell them to stop building. But are you absolutely sure about this? Your costs can double as well."

Nikola responds, "With Morgan behind me, I have never been more sure of anything."

They go outside. White speaks to the foreman, who waves the workers to stop.

* * *

A year later, the laboratory building is under construction. Nikola and a group of people are celebrating that the tower is finished. Nikola announces, "I've named the site Wardenclyffe and I envision employing two thousand people at the World Broadcasting System."

The mayor is pleased. He says, "We look forward to your success and will be intrigued watching the tower being completed."

Transmitting Tesla Tower and Laboratory built in 1901-1905
by H. Stanford White, architect and Tesla's friend.

Chapter 11

CONTROVERSIAL ISSUES

The following year, a banquet is being held in New York for Lord Kelvin, England's famous inventor, who is a dear friend of Nikola Tesla. People are milling around. Lord Kelvin, Nikola, and a small group are carrying on a conversation.

Kelvin is speaking. "I agree wholeheartedly with Tesla on two controversial issues. One, that Mars was signaling America, and two, that the conservation of renewable resources is of critical importance to the world. Windmills should be placed on roofs at the earliest opportunity to run elevators, pump water, and cool and heat houses."

A guest responds, "Edison doesn't agree. He feels we have another fifty-thousand years before the forests of South America are depleted."

"There are few of us that disagree with Edison. I must proclaim New York is the most marvelously lit city in the world, and probably the only spot on earth visible to the Martians," says Kelvin.

Nikola joins in. "Half the time I am a man condemned to death because of my views, and half the time the happiest of mortals. All is still but hope. It may take centuries, but I feel it in every fiber it is coming for sure!"

The next day's newspaper headlines read, "Mars is signaling…to New York." A man walks by the newsstand shaking his head. "Sounds like Tesla again."

A few days later, Nikola and Scherff are discussing their financial woes. Nikola says, "Morgan's one-hundred-fifty-thousand dollars is gone. I must put out something commercial to bring in some money."

"I have a few thousand I can loan until we get an income," says Scherff.

"I appreciate that. We'll complete the therapeutic oscillator for the medical profession. Doctors and professors from all over the country have been reminding me of its importance. Also, let's put on a fireworks display from the tower to prove we've got what it takes."

A few nights later, reporters are rushing to the scene, but are turned away. The flashes from the tower are awesome, brightening the night sky with the cracks that can be heard from a distance.

Headlines on the newsstand the next day read, "Tesla's Flashes Startling, But He Won't Tell What He is Trying For at Wardenclyffe."

In the Johnsons' living room, Katherine is reading from the newspaper to Robert. "For a time, the air was filled with blinding streaks of electricity which seemed to shoot off into the darkness on some mysterious errand."

Robert says, "Good grief, Katherine, Nikki is really hitting the headlines."

"Let me send him a note to see if he'll join us at the Hawthorne's next month. I miss him so much."

Robert agrees, "I guess I do, too. We've been through so much together."

* * *

J. P. Morgan's yacht is moored in New York Harbor. He often stays there instead of returning to his Madison Avenue home. He is sitting in the cabin playing solitaire as Nikola enters.

"Good morning, Mr. Morgan. I'm sorry to bother you at such a difficult time."

"What is it, Tesla?"

"Mr. Morgan, you have raised great waves in the financial world, and some have struck my little boat. The crash on Wall Street has affected so many of us; the panic has abolished my credit and created costly delays. I need more funds at once or Wardenclyffe will close down."

Morgan replies, "I gave you the agreed upon figure, which was Fifty-thousand-dollars more than you requested."

"But my plans were based on costs in a normal economy. Prices skyrocketed. This was not taken into account when we began," says Nikola.

"Let me see those bills." He looks them over. "This tower is 187 feet high!"

"Yes sir, it is," responds Nikola.

"I don't understand. Your plan was for a ninety-foot tower."

"Yes, I know, Mr. Morgan, but…"

"But what?"

"Marconi pirated my radio. I had to destroy the thief."

"You doubled the size of the tower and you're blaming ME for cost overruns. Is that correct?" asks Morgan sternly. He focuses a long, icily unreal stare at Nikola.

"Perhaps I should come at another time." Obviously shaken, Nikola gathers up his papers and hastily exits.

A few nights later, H. Stanford White is in his office. He is working on blueprints for a mansion. He hears sounds at the door and looks up, frightened. Knocks on the door echo eerily. He pulls a pistol from a drawer. "Who is it?"

"It's me, Ann," says Ann Morgan.

White unlocks and opens the door.

"I heard from Daddy's secretary about a horrendous argument with Nikki. I know there can never be anything between us, even though I think the world of him, but his work is more important to me than my feelings."

White responds, "His vision could still produce great work."

"Daddy's so stubborn. You're the only one who ever changes his mind. Just have him void their contract, or something."

"I've got a plan. Your father's a bulwark, sure, but he realizes his war on Harriman topped Wall Street. There's more than one way to skin a grizzly."

Ann laughs nervously and hands White an envelope. "Please give this to Nikki, but DON'T reveal the source."

White nods. "I understand. Chin up. If we turn the bear around we'll make the history books."

Ann musters a smile and leaves.

A few days later at Wardenclyffe, Nikola is outside taking measurements. White pulls up in his new car. "I heard about the wrangling between you and Morgan. I have this for you. Hope it will get you to where you want to go."

"Thanks for the loan, Stanford," says Nikola. "I won't forget it."

"It isn't from me, but return it to me when you can. I have a plan, a long shot, to turn Morgan around."

Nikola says, "He's blocking me from other investors."

"I'll give it my best shot. He's sore at you for changing the plans, but when he sees this tower we can't miss."

Nikola, quite a bit more cheerful, says, "I feel like Prometheus, the Titan who stole the sacred fire of the gods and gave it to the struggling, suffering humans of this world, only to be chained to a rock and punished by Zeus."

White's gaze joins Nikola's as the wizard stares intently up at the peak of the tower. Nikola's thoughts have already drifted to a level beyond the mundane matters of the world. White pats him on the back and leaves.

Chapter 12

TESLA'S FINANCIAL CRISIS

In Westinghouse's Pittsburgh office, Nikola is showing him photographs of his Wardenclyffe Tower, the laboratory, and a prospectus. Westinghouse's response is guarded. "Most impressive, Nikola, most impressive. Thanks for considering the Westinghouse Corporation, and good luck with it."

"I've been crushed in the panic, George. I'm scraping the bottom of the barrel, yet this project is worth two-hundred-thousand dollars. With only fifty-thousand dollars more, I can complete my World Broadcasting Center. With its wireless communication, my AC revenues will pale in comparison."

Westinghouse responds, "I'm sure you're right, but I can't join you in this venture. It's taken us from the day we bought your patents until now to pay off the hundred-million-dollar debt."

"Most of that was spent on legalities, George!"

"You tell that to our creditors. We're presently quite unable to go into ANY other enterprise."

Nikola sounds desperate. "I'll be blunt, George. I believe you owe me. In your time of crisis I destroyed a contract worth twenty times more than what I'm asking from you now. Was our relationship merely business?"

"I'd help you if I could, but I can't. I'm just a powerless figurehead now. The board forced me out."

Nikola softens. "I'm sorry. I didn't know."

"I told them that we were investing in America. The truth is, I'm only kept on for advertising purposes and worker morale. I can loan a few thousand out of my pocket, but my 'wealth' is locked up in company stock."

Now almost depressed, Nikola says, "This is a very sad day, George. I don't want YOUR money."

At the Waldorf Astoria Hotel, where Nikola has been living for twenty years, the manager, Mr. Boldt, gestures him into the back office. "It pains me to bring this up, Mr. Tesla, but your rent is late again. I am forced to seize your assets."

"My good man, we have known each other for twenty years. Have I not paid my rent for nineteen of them?"

"Yes, you've paid for nineteen of them."

"With the war and the financial crash, it is taking me much longer to recover from the debts. Can you wait a little bit longer?"

Boldt answers, "Only until the end of the month."

Eventually, the Yugoslavian government intervenes and helps Nikola pay for a place to stay.

In Nikola's laboratory he appears haggard, and his usually neat laboratory is quite messy. His laboratory is now a warehouse. He drags himself to a table, hooks up some electric wires to his wrists, and then sends electricity through his body. He shakes his head and appears to have regained some energy. He has aged quite a bit. Czito, who is still his loyal assistant, turns to him and says, "Sir, what can I do to help you?"

"Not much right now," answers Nikola. "My beautiful white pigeon with the grey tips on her wings became ill and died. We have truly loved each other for a very long time. She always came to me, and I brought her to the apartment to nurse her when she was ill."

"I know how important the pigeons are to you," says Czito.

"But, Czito, she was always that very special one. I feel much better now. Let's get to work."

Later, Edison and Tesla are nominated for a Nobel Peace Price in Stockholm, Sweden. Nikola does not attend to pick up his prize. One of the officials is reading a letter from him. "Tesla is declining to attend. He's unclear why, but I heard through the grapevine it's because Edison is also being honored."

* * *

At Wardenclyffe in 1917, the tower is being dismantled for salvage to satisfy Nikola's debts. The destroyers have to keep blasting away because the tower proves stronger than they anticipated. Dynamite is being used, and a junk man notices some of Nikola's notes blowing down the street. The junk man picks up one of the notes. He is reading the letters. "I did not exactly cry when I saw my place after so long an interval, but I came very close."

It is now 1937, and a government official is visiting Nikola. They are deep in conversation. "War is eminent. The aggression of Germany is felt all over Europe. We need to be prepared in everyway possible."

"Many of my inventions are available for defense purposes," says Nikola. "My teleautomata can replace man where danger is eminent."

"I heard you and Einstein were working on experiments for transporting people in time and space."

"Well," answers Nikola, "we've developed some calculations and we're both in agreement it can happen. I have some basic apparatus I've developed over the years."

"The government would like to buy what you have available. This could be quite a defensive tactic, both on land and at sea."

Nikola says, "It's not perfected yet. But I would suggest you start with a shipboard experiment. We believe both man and objects will disappear from the radar screen."

There is a slight pause, and the government official says, "Maybe our timing will come together. We have our scientists working on this type of experiment."

* * *

Nikola is poverty-stricken and won't attend a function held at the Biltmore on May 12, 1938, given by The Institute of Immigrant Welfare in his honor. He sends a speech to be read on his behalf.

"Mr. Tesla could not attend this evening, but sent the following to be read to all of you in his absence...'George Westinghouse was, in my opinion, the only man on this globe who could take my alternating-current system under the circumstances then existing and win the battle against prejudice and money power. He was a pioneer of imposing stature, one of the world's true noblemen of whom America may well be proud and to whom humanity owes an immense debt of gratitude.' "

It is now the end of 1942. World War II is raging. The Christmas lights are still bright as Nikola turns the calendar to 1943. He is eighty-seven years old and in frail health. He walks to the window of his laboratory and sees a thunderstorm with lightning flashes in the wintry sky. "I have made better lightning than that."

People are walking with turned-up collars. Scherff comes to assist with an experiment. Suddenly, Nikola clutches his heart as a sharp pain stabs his chest. "Come, let's go to a doctor," says Scherff.

Nikola sits down. "No, no, no. I'll be fine."

In a short time he rallies and rises from the couch. "I'm going home early tonight."

Scherff says, "Let me go with you."

"No, no, no," Nikola insists.

LEGACY

He stops to feed the pigeons. He talks to some of them by name and they respond as if he were an old friend.

The next day in his hotel room, the maid knocks on the door. Pigeons are perched on the windowsill. Nikola opens the door.

"Time to straighten up your room, Mr. Tesla," says the maid.

"Okay, but please see that I get no visitors today. I must not be disturbed."

The maid dusts and straightens up while he tends to the pigeons. When she leaves, he puts out a "Do Not Disturb" sign.

The following day, the maid knocks and there is no answer. She knocks again, then disregards the "Do Not Disturb" sign and, using her pass key, enters the room. Nikola Tesla has been dead for hours. The calendar on the wall reads January 8, 1943.

A few days later, more than two thousand people file into the aisles of the church. A flag of his adopted country is used. The Serbs and the Croats seat themselves on opposite sides of the cathedral. A hush settles over the crowd as footsteps cease. A eulogy is given by one of the respected men in the scientific community.

"Tesla was a world-class citizen. The recipient of three Nobel Prizes in Physics, he is indeed one of the outstanding intellects of the world who paved the way for many of the technological developments of our time."

# # # #

Tesla Funeral on January 12, 1943.

Nikola Tesla was the discoverer of alternating current, and the father of radar, robotics, and wireless transmission. Our world owes him much for his visions, his struggles, and his quest to make the world a better place for mankind.

The Yugoslavian government paid to have a beautiful statue of Nikola Tesla put on Goat Island at Niagara Falls in New York. A Tesla Museum was also built in Belgrade.

HERE DIED, ON JANUARY 7, 1943, AT THE AGE OF 87, THE GREAT YUGOSLAV-AMERICAN SCIENTIST-INVENTOR, NIKOLA TESLA, WHOSE DISCOVERIES IN THE FIELD OF ALTERNATING ELECTRIC CURRENT ADVANCED THE UNITED STATES AND THE REST OF THE WORLD INTO THE MODERN INDUSTRIAL ERA.

YUGOSLAV-AMERICAN BICENTENNIAL COMMITTEE, JANUARY 7, 1977

Tesla commemorative plaque located on the Hotel New Yorker.

Suggested Reading

Tesla's Oscillator and Other Inventions; *Century* magazine article, April 1895.

The Problem of Increasing Human Energy by Nikola Tesla; *Century* magazine article, June 1900.

Edison, Morgan and Tesla by Daniel Blair Stewart.

The Philadelphia Experiment, Project Invisibility by William L. Moore and Charles Berlitz, Fawcett Crest, New York, 1979.

Nikola Tesla, Free Energy and the White Dove, Abelard Productions, Inc., 1992.

Prodigal Genius, The Life of Nikola Tesla by John J. O'Neill, Angriff Press, 1978.

The Niagara Falls Question & Answer Book by George Bailey, published by Royal Specialty Sales, 1998.

Nikola Tesla, and the Taming of Electricity by Lisa J. Aldrich. Morgan Reynolds Publishing, 2005.

Tesla's Experiments of Alternating Currents of Great Frequency, *Scientific American* article, March 26, 1892, p. 195.

Nikola Tesla's Latest Invention, *Scientific American* article, November 19, 1898, p. 326.

Tesla's Wireless Light, *Scientific American* article, February 2, 1901, p. 67.

LEGACY

Tesla, Man of Mystery by Michael X, Inner Light Publications, 1992.

Nikola Tesla, *Colorado Springs Notes*, 1899-1900, Nolit, Beograd, Yugoslavia, 1978.

Nikola Tesla, *Electrical Journal* articles, September 1890– December 1933.

Occult Ether Physics: Tesla's Hidden Space Propulsion System and the Conspiracy to Conceal It by William Lyne.

Some Patent Applications of Nikola Tesla, 1916-1920.

Tesla, The Lost Inventions by George Trinkaus, 1988.

Tesla Coil by George Trinkaus, 1989.

Radio Tesla by George Trinkaus, 1993.

Tesla: Man out of Time by Margaret Cheney, Dell Publishing, 1981.

Nikola Tesla, World's Greatest Engineer by Commander E. J. Quinby (USN, Ret.), Proceeding of the Radio Club of America, Inc., Fall 1971.

Available at www.amazon.com

Made in the USA
Lexington, KY
07 July 2010